COLLEGE GOATs

THE GREATEST OF ALL TIME

GOATs OF COLLEGE SOFTBALL

BY HALEY WILLIAMS

An Imprint of Abdo Publishing
abdobooks.com

abdobooks.com

Published by Abdo Publishing, a division of ABDO, PO Box 398166, Minneapolis, Minnesota 55439.

Printed in the United States of America, North Mankato, Minnesota.
102025
012026

Cover Photo: Sarah Stier/Getty Images Sport/Getty Images
Interior Photos: UCLA Athletics, 4, 12; Todd Warshaw/Getty Images Sport/Getty Images, 7; Doug Hoke/Time Life Pictures/Sports Illustrated/Getty Images, 8; University of Arizona Athletics, 11; Bryan Terry/NCAA Photos/Getty Images, 15; Doug Pensinger/Getty Images Sport/Getty Images, 16; Chris Landsberger/NCAA Photos/Getty Images, 18–19; Jerry Laizure/AP Images, 20; Dustin Snipes/Icon Sportswire, 23; J. P. Wilson/Icon Sportswire, 24; Shane Bevel/NCAA Photos/Getty Images, 26–27, 28–29, 31, 36, 39; Michelle Lepianka Carter/The Tuscaloosa News/AP Images, 32; Mike Janes/Four Seam Images/AP Images, 34–35; Brian Bahr/Getty Images Sport/Getty Images, 40, 43

Editor: Dalton Rains
Series Designer: Kate Liestman

Library of Congress Control Number: 2025939141

Publisher's Cataloging-in-Publication Data

Names: Williams, Haley, author.
Title: GOATS of college softball / by Haley Williams
Description: Minneapolis, Minnesota: Abdo Publishing, 2026 | Series: College GOATs: the greatest of all time | Includes online resources and index.
Identifiers: ISBN 9781098298340 (lib. bdg.) | ISBN 9798384932147 (ebook)
Subjects: LCSH: College sports--Juvenile literature. | Women college athletes--Juvenile literature. | Softball--Juvenile literature. | Sports records--Juvenile literature. | College sports--Records--Juvenile literature.
Classification: DDC 796.3578--dc23

TABLE OF CONTENTS

DOT RICHARDSON

Dot Richardson's talent on the softball diamond showed early. By age 10, she had started playing in an adult league in her hometown of Orlando, Florida. Three years later, in 1975, she joined the Orlando Rebels. They were a professional team in the Women's Major Fastpitch League. Richardson was the youngest person ever to play in the league. Her career was just getting started.

Richardson grew up during an important time in girls' and women's sports. Boys used to have many more opportunities to play sports than girls did. In 1972, the US government passed a law called Title IX.

In 2006, former UCLA infielder Dot Richardson was inducted into the USA Softball Hall of Fame.

It prevented people from being excluded from school activities based on their sex. Before Title IX, players usually had to organize softball teams themselves. Some schools didn't allow women's sports at all. After Title IX, many schools formed softball teams. Women such as Richardson got more opportunities to play college sports.

Richardson wanted to play at the University of California, Los Angeles (UCLA). The Bruins were a powerhouse in college softball. However, Richardson didn't get an offer to join the team. So in 1980, the middle infielder started playing at the smaller Western Illinois University.

In her freshman season, Richardson led the nation with a .480 batting average. Her play finally caught the attention of the UCLA coaches. She transferred for the 1981 season. Richardson led the team in batting average in each of her three seasons with the Bruins. In 1982, she lifted the team to the Women's College World Series (WCWS). They went undefeated in the tournament on the way to their first national championship under the National College Athletic Association (NCAA). Richardson was later named the NCAA Player of the Decade for the 1980s.

FAST FACT

In 1996, softball was added to the Olympics. Richardson was one of the stars of the United States' team. She hit a home run that clinched the gold medal. Richardson played with the national team for more than two decades and won another Olympic gold medal in 2000.

MICHELE SMITH

Growing up in New Jersey, Michele Smith played a lot of sports. When she wasn't playing basketball or field hockey, she worked hard to become a softball pitcher. The southpaw finished her high school career with school records for strikeouts, no-hitters, and wins. After visiting Oklahoma State, she immediately knew she wanted to play there.

However, Smith's softball career almost ended after her freshman year. On July 21, 1986, she was driving home from an appointment with her father. He was steering around a turn when the passenger door suddenly opened. Smith fell out of the car and collided with a post, causing a devasting elbow injury to her pitching arm.

Smith had surgery and went through nine months of rehabilitation. But even her doctors didn't believe she would ever pitch again. Yet she did just that. In fact, she was able to pitch faster than ever.

In 1989, the resilient Smith left Oklahoma State with an 82–20 record, 600 strikeouts, and a 0.75 earned-run average (ERA). Meanwhile, at the plate, she recorded a career .343 batting average, 15 home runs, and 87 runs batted in (RBIs).

FAST FACT

Michele Smith played in softball's debut Olympics. On July 21, 1996, she took the field against Puerto Rico exactly 10 years after her injury. The United States won 10–0 and eventually won the gold medal.

Former Oklahoma State pitcher Michele Smith competes with Team USA in 1995.

Lisa Fernandez had a 93–7 pitching record at UCLA.

LISA FERNANDEZ

Lisa Fernandez is considered one of the best softball players of all time. She worked hard for that legacy. The daughter of two athletes, Fernandez started playing from a young age in California. Her mom taught her how to pitch and often helped her practice.

As a kid, Fernandez was told that her arms weren't long enough for her to play at an elite level. But thanks in part to her mother's encouragement, Fernandez didn't quit. She eventually became a star pitcher on her high school team. In four years, she posted an incredible 0.07 ERA. She also threw 37 no-hitters and 12 perfect games. Those stats caught the attention of UCLA coaches.

Starting as a freshman in 1990, Fernandez dominated college competition. In the circle, her changeup often froze batters. And her rise balls made hard-to-hit jumps into the strike zone. That helped her record a 0.22 career ERA, the second lowest in NCAA history. Fernandez was also a force at the plate. As a senior in 1993, she recorded an NCAA-leading .510 with 11 home runs and 45 RBIs.

By the time she left college in 1993, Fernandez had lifted the Bruins to four straight WCWS appearances. Two of those appearances ended with national championships. In 1993, she became the first softball player to be named Collegiate Woman Athlete of the Year for all sports.

Graduation wasn't the end of Fernandez's softball career. From 1996 to 2004, she helped the United States win three straight Olympic gold medals. She also coached at UCLA for more than 20 years.

JENNY DALTON

From 1993 to 1996, Jenny Dalton was one of the most feared batters in college softball. The California native played for legendary coach Mike Candrea at Arizona. During that time, she set multiple NCAA records. These included a single-season record of 101 runs scored and a career-record 328 RBIs. Her 293 career runs scored also stood as a record for 20 years.

The second baseman helped Arizona win back-to-back national championships in 1993 and 1994. In 1995, the Wildcats were looking to become the second team in history to three-peat as champions. However, a 4–2 loss to rival UCLA in the final dashed their hopes.

Not to be discouraged, Dalton finished her career on a high note. In 1996, the All-America senior became the first player in Pacific-10 (Pac-10) Conference history to win the Triple Crown. She did that by leading the NCAA with a .469 batting average, 25 home runs, and 109 RBIs. She also earned national player of the year honors.

To cap off her college career, Dalton helped Arizona make it back to the WCWS for the fourth time. The Wildcats went undefeated in

FAST FACT

After college, Dalton—now Dalton-Hill—focused her efforts on baseball. She played for the Colorado Silver Bullets, a professional women's baseball team. She also became a member of the US Women's National Baseball Team.

the tournament. After blasting a three-run homer in the championship game, Dalton won her third title and was named the WCWS Most Outstanding Player (MOP).

Arizona went 232–26 during Jenny Dalton's college career.

Stacey Nuveman finished her UCLA career with a .945 slugging percentage.

STACEY NUVEMAN

Starting in 1997, Stacey Nuveman added her name to the long list of dominant UCLA softball players. The catcher began her college career with a bang. As a freshman, she led the Bruins in batting average, home runs, RBIs, and slugging percentage. Nuveman also set the team's single-season home run record with 20. She earned the Pac-10 Newcomer of the Year award for her efforts.

An injury forced Nuveman to take a redshirt season in 1998. She came back in the 1999 season as dominant as ever. She racked up a .446 batting average with a 1.016 slugging percentage and 91 RBIs. Her 31 home runs were an NCAA record at the time. Nuveman also led the Bruins to an undefeated run at the WCWS. UCLA beat Washington 3–2 to win the program's eighth national championship.

In 2000, Nuveman wanted to compete at the Olympic Games in Sydney, Australia, with the US Women's National Team. The NCAA gave her permission to redshirt again. Although she was the youngest member of the team, Nuveman proved her worth in the semifinals. She hit a home run to clinch a win in extra innings. Another victory gave Nuveman her first gold medal. She went on to win another gold and a silver at the next two Games.

Nuveman came back to UCLA in 2001 and 2002. As a senior, she showcased her power at the plate. She led the nation with a .529 batting average and a .665 on-base percentage. Nuveman broke four NCAA career records as well. She finished with 240 walks, with 81 being intentional, and she had 90 home runs.

JENNIE FINCH

Five-year-old Jennie Finch couldn't wait to start playing T-ball. Growing up with two older brothers and parents who loved baseball, the California native always had a passion for sports. Her father even built a batting cage in her family's backyard. At the age of eight, Finch began pitching. Right away, her hand-eye coordination and powerful arm were clear to see.

Finch played at Arizona from 1999 to 2002. The 6-foot pitcher recorded an ERA of less than 1.00 in three of her four seasons. Between April 29, 2000, and April 6, 2002, she won 60 consecutive games in the circle. That set an NCAA record. Finch was also a strong hitter. She batted above .300 in three seasons and had 52 career home runs.

Finch's best season came in 2001. The lights-out pitcher gave up only 16 runs through 207 innings. Her ERA was 0.54. Finch also went a perfect 32–0, which set another NCAA record. She helped Arizona to an undefeated run in the WCWS. In the championship, Finch pitched a 1–0 shutout against UCLA to clinch the Wildcats' sixth title. Afterward, she was named the tournament's MOP.

Finch left college as a two-time national player of the year. However, her softball career was just beginning. As part of the US Women's National Team, she won Olympic gold and silver medals. She also played in the National Pro Fastpitch (NPF) league.

Arizona's Jennie Finch was a three-time All-America pitcher and first baseman.

Jessica Mendoza sprints toward home plate during the 2004 Olympic Games.

JESSICA MENDOZA

As a freshman in 1999, Jessica Mendoza batted .415 with 81 hits. Nine of those were home runs. She also drove in 57 runs for Stanford. Those stats helped Mendoza become Stanford's first National Fastpitch Coaches Association (NFCA) first-team All-American. Her performance also sparked a new period of success for the Cardinal.

Mendoza went on to earn first-team All-America honors in all four of her seasons at Stanford. As a sophomore in 2000, she recorded a career-high .475 average, 94 hits, and 20 doubles. The next season, Mendoza led Stanford to its first-ever WCWS appearance. Then she finished her college career in 2002 by recording team-high numbers in nearly every hitting category. The Cardinal legend left college as Stanford's all-time leader in batting average, hits, home runs, runs scored, and stolen bases.

Competing on the US Women's National Team, Mendoza went on to win gold at the 2004 Olympics in Athens, Greece. Then she won silver at the 2008 Games in Beijing, China. She also became a trailblazing television analyst. In 2007, she became one of ESPN's lead commentators for college softball alongside fellow legend Michele Smith and broadcaster Beth Mowins.

Mendoza made more history in 2015. She became the first female analyst to provide commentary for a nationally televised Major League Baseball (MLB) game. She also became the first woman to commentate an MLB postseason game.

NATASHA WATLEY

In the late 1900s, softball players started using a technique called slap hitting. Slapping is when a hitter runs at the pitch as the ball speeds toward the plate. This allows the hitter to get a quicker start out of the batter's box. By the early 2000s, the strategy was rising in popularity. Few players did it better than Natasha Watley.

Watley played at UCLA from 2000 to 2003. During that time, the speedy shortstop was one of the toughest outs in college softball. In 2001, Watley went on a 32-game hitting streak. The following year, she had 112 hits. That number remained among the NCAA's top 10 for single-season hits for more than two decades.

However, Watley saved her best for last. She led UCLA to the WCWS in 2003. There, she posted a tournament-leading .462 batting average on the way to a national championship.

The 2003 title added to Watley's many accomplishments. She ended her career as one of the most prolific offensive players in UCLA history. Watley set Bruins records for career hits, triples, and runs scored. She also led the team in steals for four straight years, leaving college with a UCLA-record 158 swiped bags. After her senior season, Watley became just the second softball player to be named the Collegiate Woman Athlete of the Year for all sports.

UCLA infielder Natasha Watley, *right*, was a four-time All-American.

Pitcher Cat Osterman led the Texas Longhorns to three WCWS appearances between 2003 and 2006.

CAT OSTERMAN

By the time Texas native Cat Osterman graduated from high school, she had already shown signs of the star she'd soon become. The pitcher once struck out 33 hitters in a 14-inning game. Every major college program wanted her. But her dream was to play for the University of Texas.

Osterman began playing with the Longhorns in 2002. She didn't pitch with a ton of speed. But she used drop pitches to get the ball past hitters. The southpaw posted a 136–25 career record from 2002 to 2006. She was named the Big 12 Conference Pitcher of the Year in each of her four college seasons. She recorded the nation's lowest ERA in three of those seasons. By the end of her career, she held several NCAA records. These included her nine perfect games. The historic player earned national player of the year honors three times.

Osterman redshirted in 2004 to compete with the US Women's National Team at the Olympics. It was the first of three trips to the Games. Osterman won a gold medal and two silvers. She retired in 2021 as one of the most decorated pitchers in softball history.

FAST FACT

The Athletes Unlimited pro sports league has a unique format. Players switch teams each week and earn points based on their individual performance. In 2020, Osterman became the league's first softball champion.

CAITLIN LOWE

As a kid, Caitlin Lowe dreamed of playing for the New York Yankees. The California native wanted to be the team's center fielder. Even though she ended up playing softball instead of baseball, she still had a passion for the outfield.

While competing for Arizona from 2004 to 2007, Lowe was one of the nation's most reliable defensive players. Over four seasons, she held a perfect 1.000 fielding percentage. Her offensive game was strong too. Batting in the leadoff spot, Lowe was a dangerous slap hitter. As a freshman, she posted a .437 average. She also stole 47 bases. She was named the 2004 Pac-10 Newcomer of the Year.

Lowe kept up the momentum as a sophomore in 2005. She recorded 100 hits off a .510 batting average. In 2006, Lowe missed part of the season due to a hand injury. But she came back in time to help the Wildcats win a national championship that year. Arizona followed that up with its second straight title in 2007.

After college, the center fielder went on to dominate in international competition. During the 2008 Games in Beijing, China, she recorded the first Olympic inside-the-park home run. The United States won a silver medal that year.

In 2012, Lowe joined the staff at Arizona under her former coach Mike Candrea. Candrea retired in 2021. After that, Lowe took over as head coach of the legendary program.

Arizona's Caitlin Lowe made the All-WCWS team in 2006 and 2007.

MONICA ABBOTT

California native Monica Abbott started playing softball when she was around six years old. At first, she played catcher. But receiving fast pitches scared her. Abbott's coach asked if she wanted

Tennessee's Monica Abbott was the first Division 1 softball pitcher with more than 500 strikeouts in four different seasons.

to try pitching instead. Things clicked for the young player. Soon, it was the opposing batters' turn to be afraid.

By high school, Abbott dominated in the circle. The 6-foot-3 southpaw posted more than 300 strikeouts each season. She became one of the nation's most sought-after recruits and eventually picked Tennessee.

From 2004 to 2007, Abbott's speed and control made her a lights-out collegiate pitcher. She set NCAA records in several pitching categories. The records included career wins, shutouts, and innings pitched. She also broke the single-season strikeout record with 724 and the career strikeout record with 2,440.

By the end of her college career, Abbott was the most decorated softball player in Lady Volunteers history. She led Tennessee to three WCWS appearances, including its first-ever in 2005. Abbott was also the first player to win the Southeastern Conference (SEC) Pitcher of the Year award three times. As a senior in 2007, she earned national player of the year honors. She later helped the United States win two Olympic silver medals.

FAST FACT

In 2012, Monica Abbott threw a 77-mile-per-hour (124-km/h) pitch during a professional game. That was the fastest softball pitch ever thrown. The record wasn't broken until 2025, when Tennessee ace Karlyn Pickens topped 78 miles per hour (126 km/h) for the first time.

DANIELLE LAWRIE

Danielle Lawrie grew up in British Columbia, Canada. She often practiced baseball with her father and brother. Lawrie's dad knew his daughter was talented. But he also knew there weren't a lot of opportunities for Lawrie to play baseball. So she switched to softball.

By the end of high school, Lawrie was one of the nation's top recruits. After touring the University of Washington, she knew it was the school for her. One perk was that the campus was close enough for her family to come to games.

Starting in 2006, Lawrie was a dominant dual-threat player for the Huskies. The right-handed pitcher threw more than 400 strikeouts in three different seasons. Meanwhile, at the plate, she hit 32 career homers and 121 RBIs. She also competed internationally while in college. She redshirted in 2008 to play for Canada at the Olympics.

Lawrie's breakout college season came in 2009. That year, the Huskies made a run to the WCWS. Lawrie pitched in each of the team's six tournament games. And she hit a grand slam in the semifinals to lift Washington to the finals. In Game 1 of the championship series, she threw a shutout against No. 1 Florida. In Game 2, the Huskies beat the Gators 3–2 to win their first national championship. Lawrie ended the tournament with 49 strikeouts and a 5–1 pitching record. She earned the WCWS MOP award to go along with her national player of the year honors.

Pitcher Danielle Lawrie was the first Washington player to win back-to-back USA Softball Collegiate Player of the Year honors.

Oklahoma pitcher Keilani Ricketts hits a home run against Tennessee in the 2013 WCWS finals.

KEILANI RICKETTS

The youngest of four children, Keilani Ricketts grew up around sports. Each of her three older siblings played college sports. Ricketts was a top softball and basketball player at her high school in San Jose, California. When it came time for college, she decided to follow in her older sister Samantha's footsteps and play at Oklahoma.

Starting in 2010, Ricketts became one of the best hitters and pitchers in Oklahoma history. She led the Sooners to three straight WCWS, including back-to-back appearances in the championship series. After losing in the 2012 finals, the Sooners won in 2013. It was the team's first national title in 13 years. Ricketts drove in all four runs in the championship-clinching win, including a three-run homer. She also finished the tournament with a perfect 4–0 record in the circle. Her dominant play earned her WCWS MOP.

Ricketts broke several Oklahoma pitching records, including career highs for wins and strikeouts. She earned national player of the year honors twice. And in 2013, she became the first Oklahoma athlete to be named Collegiate Woman Athlete of the Year for all sports.

Ricketts's softball career didn't end when she left the Sooners. She played professionally in the United States and Japan. And in 2025, she was part of the first season of the Athletes Unlimited Softball League.

LAUREN HAEGER

As a freshman, Florida right-hander Lauren Haeger posted a 1.85 ERA with 129 strikeouts. She only got better. The Peoria, Arizona, native was a four-year starter for Florida. From 2012 to 2015, she cemented herself as one of the best hitting pitchers in NCAA history.

Haeger posted 18 homers and 70 RBIs as a sophomore in 2013. Then, as a junior, she led Florida to the 2014 WCWS. She pitched three innings and posted three hits in a 6–3 Gators win to clinch the program's first national championship.

The following year, Florida made another run to the WCWS. Once again, Haeger stepped up big time. The senior posted a WCWS-leading .571 batting average with three home runs. She was just as good in the circle. Her 4–1 record on 20 strikeouts helped Florida secure its second straight WCWS title. Haeger was named the tournament's MOP.

The national championships were just two of Haeger's many accomplishments. She finished her college career with pitching win totals and home run totals higher than 70. The only other person in Division I softball, Division I baseball, or Major League Baseball to do that was baseball legend Babe Ruth. In 2015, Haeger was named the SEC Female Athlete of the Year and earned national player of the year honors.

In 2025, pitcher Lauren Haeger was inducted into the Florida Athletic Hall of Fame.

Haylie McCleney posted a .447 career batting average with Alabama.

HAYLIE McCLENEY

Growing up in Morris, Alabama, Haylie "Haylo" McCleney's backyard was a competitive space. She and her two brothers were constantly trying to prove how athletic they were. The future softball star was always trying to be the best.

When it was time for college, McCleney decided to make her mark at nearby University of Alabama. Excelling both at the plate and in the field, McCleney's all-around abilities helped her earn All-America honors all four years from 2013 to 2016. She was known for being a clutch hitter. Meanwhile, her speed and ability to make diving plays in center field made her a tough defender. The outfielder lifted Alabama to an SEC regular season championship in 2014. That year, she drove in two of the Crimson Tide's three runs in the WCWS championship series. It was one of her three WCWS appearances.

Although she never won a national championship with the Crimson Tide, McCleney set several Alabama records. Those included her career .569 on-base percentage and 16 triples. She also finished in the top 10 in several other categories. These included walks, hits, runs scored, slugging percentage, and stolen bases.

McCleney played more than 10 years with the US Women's National Team. In 2021, she recorded nine hits across six games at the Olympic Games in Tokyo, Japan. Her .529 batting average led the tournament and helped the United States win silver.

SIERRA ROMERO

Sierra Romero first stepped onto the field as a Michigan Wolverine in 2013. It was soon clear that she was going to do great things. The middle infielder from Murrieta, California, solidified herself as one of college softball's greatest hitters.

As a freshman, Romero posted a batting average of .385. In each of the following three seasons, her batting average was higher than .400. That included hitting .491 as a sophomore in 2014. In 682 career appearances at the plate, she struck out just 63 times.

By the time she left college, Romero became the first player in NCAA history to record 300 or more runs, hits, and RBIs in college. Her 302 career runs scored stood as a college record for eight years. Of her 82 career home runs, 11 were grand slams. That was also an NCAA record.

Along the way, Romero led the Wolverines to three WCWS appearances. They finished as the runners-up in 2015. That year, Romero hit a game-tying homer in the semifinals. She also drove in Michigan's only run of Game 3 of the championship series. Romero earned national player of the year honors in 2015 and again in 2016.

After college, Romero played professionally in the NPF. A knee injury in 2019 kept her off the field for more than a year. But she eventually recovered and started playing for Athletes Unlimited alongside her younger sister Sydney Romero.

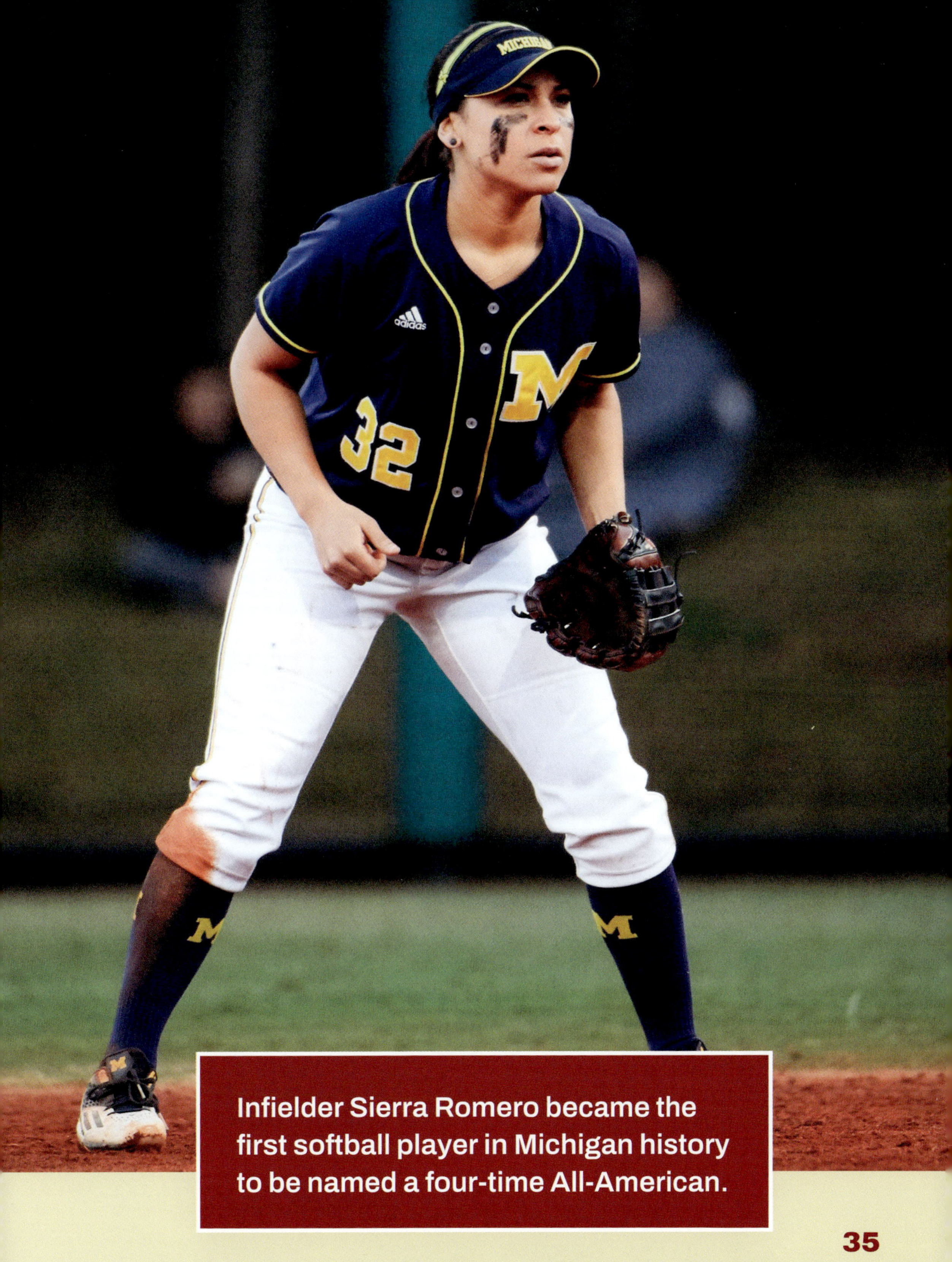

Infielder Sierra Romero became the first softball player in Michigan history to be named a four-time All-American.

Florida State third baseman Jessi Warren won back-to-back ACC Player of the Year honors in 2017 and 2018.

JESSI WARREN

Jessi Warren grew up playing baseball in Tampa, Florida. She dreamed of one day competing in the major leagues. However, no woman had ever played in the majors. So she decided to switch to softball in high school. Now, her dreams shifted to professional softball.

Warren stayed close to home for college. The third baseman began playing at Florida State in 2015. She quickly became a game changer for the Seminoles. As a freshman, Warren led her team with 11 doubles, 19 home runs, and a .761 slugging percentage. Her performance that season earned her the Atlantic Coast Conference (ACC) Freshman of the Year award.

Warren's huge showings continued over the next three seasons. Her senior year was the most impressive of all. That season, Florida State made its first-ever appearance in the WCWS. In Game 1 against Washington, Warren made a diving catch and threw out the runner at first for a double play. It became one of the most memorable plays in WCWS history. Meanwhile, at the plate, her 13 hits tied a tournament record. Her defining performances helped the Seminoles become the first ACC team to win a softball national championship. And Warren was honored as the tournament's MOP.

After college, Warren's dreams of becoming a pro softball player came true. She played four years in the NPF. In 2020, she joined Athletes Unlimited. She was named the league's Defensive Player of the Year in 2023.

RACHEL GARCIA

UCLA was a great fit for California native Rachel Garcia. The Bruins' softball program was one of the most dominant in NCAA history. So the competitive Garcia got to join one of the nation's best programs while staying close to home.

Garcia redshirted in 2016 due to a left knee injury. After that, the right-handed pitcher spent the next three seasons excelling both in the circle and at the plate. In 2019, she struck out 286 batters on her way to a 29–1 record. Meanwhile, she piled up 35 walks and 57 RBIs as a hitter.

UCLA made a run to the 2019 WCWS. In Game 1 of the championship series against Oklahoma, Garcia hit a two-run homer to put her team up 11–1. She finished the tournament with five pitching victories. Her performance in the second game of the WCWS clinched UCLA's first national championship in nine years.

In 2020, the NCAA gave permission for Garcia to redshirt again so she could compete at the Olympics. However, the COVID-19 pandemic shortened the college softball season. It also pushed the Games to 2021. Garcia decided to compete at UCLA while training

FAST FACT

The 2019 softball national title was UCLA's 12th. That was the most national championships of any team. Those titles include college softball's first three-peat from 1988 to 1990.

for the Olympics. The senior had another fantastic year. At the end of the season, she became the first softball player to win consecutive Collegiate Woman Athlete of the Year awards.

UCLA pitcher Rachel Garcia was named the 2019 WCWS MOP.

JOCELYN ALO

Jocelyn Alo's love for softball began in her hometown of Hau'ula, Hawaii. Alo's dad introduced her to the sport. The two practiced together every day.

Oklahoma's Jocelyn Alo was a four-time All-American.

Alo's father wanted to give her as many opportunities as possible. So they lived in California during summers. Alo got the opportunity to play on highly competitive club softball teams. That helped her get noticed by coaches from all the top colleges. In the end, she committed to Oklahoma.

Between 2018 and 2022, the power-hitting designated player broke several NCAA records, including highest career slugging percentage and most total bases. Alo also collected many awards as a Sooner. These included back-to-back national player of the year honors. However, Alo is best known for breaking the college home run record. After hitting 122 career bombs, she was dubbed "The Home Run Queen."

Alo's powerful swings played a big role in Oklahoma's back-to-back national titles in 2021 and 2022. During the 2022 WCWS, she posted a .667 average with 12 hits and 13 RBIs. Five of her hits were home runs. Her performance earned her tournament MOP. It also solidified her place as one of the best college hitters of all time.

FAST FACT

In 2015, Oklahoma infielder Lauren Chamberlain set the career home run record at 95. A few years later, on March 17, 2022, Jocelyn Alo broke that record. The bomb was even more special because Alo hit it in her home state of Hawaii.

TIARE JENNINGS

Since 2000, no school has enjoyed as much success as Oklahoma. And at no point were the Sooners more dominant than from 2021 to 2024. Middle infielder Tiare Jennings was a big reason for that. During the run, Oklahoma won an NCAA-record 71 straight games. The team also finished the 2023 season 61–1.

Coming in as a top recruit from San Pedro, California, Jennings made an immediate impact for the Sooners. Defensively, she was solid at second base and shortstop. She committed just 10 errors in four seasons on the way to a .983 fielding percentage.

Jennings piled up stats at the plate too. Through her career, she posted 64 doubles, 98 home runs, and 314 RBIs. Jennings also scored 277 career runs. And her batting average was more than .370 every season.

Where Jennings shone the most, though, was in the postseason. Her 87 at-bats, seven doubles, and 35 RBIs all set WCWS records. Jennings was a co-captain during her senior year in 2024.

FAST FACT

Many fans consider Oklahoma's senior class of 2024 to be the best team in softball history. In their run to four national championships, the players compiled a 235–15 record. They also had 131 run-rule wins and 114 shutout wins.

She provided leadership to her team during the biggest moments. Her calm demeanor helped the Sooners become the first NCAA softball team in history to win four straight WCWS titles.

Tiare Jennings posted a career batting average of .412 at Oklahoma.

HONORABLE MENTIONS

LEAH O'BRIEN

O'Brien helped Arizona win national championships in 1993, 1994, and 1997. The infielder also set several NCAA hitting records. Outside of college, O'Brien won three Olympic gold medals.

KELLY KRETSCHMAN

Between 1998 and 2001, Kretschman was a powerful hitter at Alabama. The shortstop and outfielder finished with a .437 career batting average and broke multiple school records, including games started, runs, slugging percentage, hits, and doubles.

SAMANTHA FINDLAY

In 2005, Michigan freshman Findlay hit a home run in the top of the 10th inning to beat UCLA 4–1 and win the WCWS. The bomb helped the Wolverines become the first team east of the Mississippi River to win a national championship.

ANGELA TINCHER

Tincher was a superstar pitcher for Virginia Tech. As a senior in 2008, she led the team to its first WCWS. She left college with a 0.78 career ERA and 2,149 total strikeouts.

DALLAS ESCOBEDO

Escobedo led Arizona State to three WCWS appearances, including an undefeated run for the national championship in 2011. The freshman pitcher was named the WCWS co-MOP that year. Escobedo threw more than 300 strikeouts in three different seasons and had a 115–26 record.

LAUREN CHAMBERLAIN

As a sophomore in 2013, Chamberlain led Oklahoma to its second national championship. The infielder finished her career with 95 home runs and a .960 slugging percentage.

KARLI SPAID

Spaid was an offensive machine at the University of Miami in Ohio from 2021 to 2024. The infielder secured her name in the NCAA record books by hitting 36 home runs in a season and blasting 103 career home runs.

GLOSSARY

analyst

In a broadcast, a person who provides details or explanations specific to the topic.

changeup

A pitch that looks like a fastball but is thrown much more slowly to deceive the hitter.

conference

A group of schools that join together to create a league for their sports teams.

earned-run average (ERA)

A statistic that measures the average number of earned runs a pitcher gives up per seven innings.

legacy

How a person or team is remembered.

recruit

An athlete whom a college team is interested in.

redshirt

To practice with a college team but not play in any games for one season.

rehabilitation

Restoring someone to health through training and therapy after an injury or illness.

resilient

Able to withstand or recover from hardship.

rival

An opponent with whom a player or team has a fierce and ongoing competition.

run rule

A college softball rule that says a game can end early if one team leads by eight runs or more after five or more innings.

slugging percentage

A measure of a player's ability to hit for power.

southpaw

A left-handed pitcher.

MORE INFORMATION

BOOKS

Big Book of Who Women in Sports: The 101 Stars Every Fan Needs to Know. Triumph, 2025.

Flynn, Brendan. *Girls' Softball*. Abdo, 2022.

Shapiro, Sean. *Everything Softball*. Abdo, 2025.

ONLINE RESOURCES

To learn more about the GOATs of college softball, please visit **abdobooklinks.com** or scan this QR code. These links are routinely monitored and updated to provide the most current information available.

INDEX

ABOUT THE AUTHOR

Haley Williams is an editor who lives in Minnesota. She played softball for 18 years, including five years in college. In her free time, she enjoys coaching club softball and going to watch college tournaments with her mom.